Strangers in Their Own Land

South Carolina's State Indian Tribes
Third Edition

S. Pony Hill

Backintyme
Palm Coast, Florida U.S.A.

Published by Backintyme,
A subsidiary of Boxes and Arrows, Inc.

Backintyme Publishing
30 Medford Drive
Palm Coast FL 32137-2504

phone: 860-468-9631
email: sales@backintyme.com
website: http://backintyme.com/publishing.php

ISBN: 978-0939479-405
Printed in the United States of America
Library of Congress Control Number: 2012956328

The cover photo is of a Sumter Cheraw family.

Contents

List of Figures

Foreword

Books about Native Americans written by non-Indian historians and anthropologists often seem boring or disinteresting to Indian people, for two reasons. First of all the books tend to be full of technical jargon and historical details which are only marginally interesting from an Indian perspective. Second, the books are often written from an Anglo historical and cultural perspective which native people frequently find to be at least annoying, or at worst downright racist.

On the other hand, books written by native people themselves, describing their own culture and history, are usually well received in the dominant society, because of their deep authenticity. No matter if a scholar from the dominant society might disagree with a native author, the author cannot be faulted for his perspective, his view from the grass roots of Indian culture. When the author has spent many years traveling to Indian communities around the Southeast and talking to Indian elders, as Pony Hill has done, he must be admired not only for his authenticity, but also for his scholarship. This book, then, is where an authentic perspective is enhanced by thorough scholarship.

The native communities around the Southeast, described by Pony Hill, are not well known to outsiders, for reasons explained by Mr. Hill. Nevertheless, they are as interesting in their own ways than the better-known Cherokees, Mvskokes and Choctaws. In addition to maintaining elements of their traditional cultures, the peoples described in this book have also developed what we might call "survival skills," overcoming their often precarious hold on a land base, and resisting the attempts of non-Indian communities and politicians to deny them the privilege of calling themselves "Indians." After many episodes of manipulation and persecution, they are still there.

There is much more to be said about each one of these Native American communities in South Carolina, and others around the Southeast. One can hope that Pony Hill and young Indian scholars inspired by him will be producing more authentic and scholarly books of this sort.

John H. Moore, Ph.D.
Anthropology Department
University of Florida
Gainesville, FL

Introduction

MODERN INDIAN TRIBES OF SOUTH CAROLINA

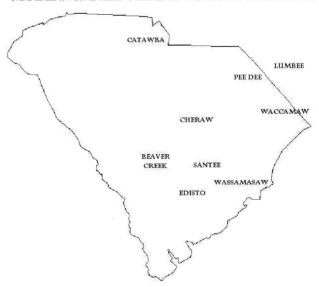

Figure 1: Modern Indian Tribes of South Carolina (Map)

Very little has been written about the Palmetto State's Indian communities since the 1960's. At that time local and state newspapers carried articles almost weekly describing the legal battles between Indian families and their county school boards over inclusion of Indian children in White schools. Since integration was completed, South Carolina's Native populations have pulled another vanishing act in the print media. Prior to 1930, writings on the subject of South Carolina's numerous Indian people are almost nonexistent.

Figure 2: Tribal dancers, UNITY pow-wow, 2009

Even when local reporters or historians mentioned Indian families or individuals, they usually left out any nod or wink as to non-White ancestry. Worse, they immortalized wild flights of fancy about the origins of their brown-skinned neighbors neighbors. To quote one amateur historian, the ancestries of their Indian citizenry were as "mysterious as the mound builders."[1] While a few renowned scholars, well versed in Native American history, did publish brief reports describing the small Indian hamlets within South Carolina's borders and their undeniable connections to larger Indian communities in North Carolina, fantastical Jules Verne style stories about escaped pirates and Lost Colony survivors still crept into local print.

Even though living side-by-side in largely rural, agricultural regions, the Indians were a clannish, strange, and inaccessible caste in the viewpoints of their White and Black neighbors, due

---

[1] *News and Courier*, Charleston SC, September 1953

in no small part to the reserved, stand-offish nature of the Indians themselves. One of the earliest mentions of these Indian people readily admits that they were willing to socialize "with neither white people nor the colored people, but prefer to keep to themselves."[2] Truly they were strangers in their own land. While Southeastern Indian people are indeed a quiet and secretive class, they have been neither invisible nor hidden. Researchers can easily find the core ancestors of any of these communities on census schedules, taxation rolls, local history books, and even local newspaper articles. Usually one will find them recorded as "Free Persons of Color" or "Other Free Persons" prior to the Civil War, "White," "Mulatto," or "Indian" up to the turn of the Century, and solidly as "Indian" thereafter. Certain surnames such as Chavis, Goins, Locklear, and Oxendine serve as red flags for tracking Indian communities across the Southeast as these surnames look as if they only appear among Indian-blooded people.

Almost all of the core ancestors of South Carolina's modern tribes (other than the Catawba) can be documented in land, taxation, and census records as migrating into the Palmetto State in two different waves. The first, or "Fishing Creek," was a wave of mixed-blood Indian families from the Fishing Creek area of Granville County, North Carolina who entered South Carolina during the 1740 to 1760 period. This wave was primarily the Braveboy, Chavis, Clark, Driggers, and Scott families. Without exception every Indian community north of Charleston counts this wave of Indian families among their ancestors. An offshoot of the Fishing Creek migration was responsible for founding the "Charraw settlement" on Drowning Creek, Robeson County.

The second, or "Drowning Creek," wave of migration were the descendents of the earlier Fishing Creek wave offshoot at Drowning Creek who, along with intermarried Indian families, made a southerly migration in the post-Revolutionary War era of

---

[2]Founding document of the Berea United Methodist Church, Dillon County SC, 1878

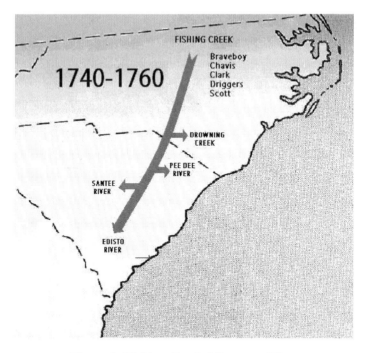

Figure 3: Fishing Creek Migratory Wave

1785 to 1820. The surnames primarily associated with this wave are Ammons, Bass, Cummings, Deas, Dimery, Hunt, Locklear, Lowry, Oxendine, Quick, Sweat, and Turner. These families left behind parents and/or siblings who had already established a thriving community on Drowning Creek and these same surnames are the core ancestors of the Indians known as "Lumbee" today. The Drowning Creek wave did not impact much further than the High Hills of Santee, and are mainly included in the ancestors of the Pee Dee, Sumter Cheraw, and Waccamaw. In reality this migratory wave lasted well over a century as Indian families from Robeson continued to move to Dillon, Horry, and Marlboro well into the 1900's. The fluidity with which the Indians moved between South Carolina and Robeson is astonishing and it becomes harder to track the families back and forth to-

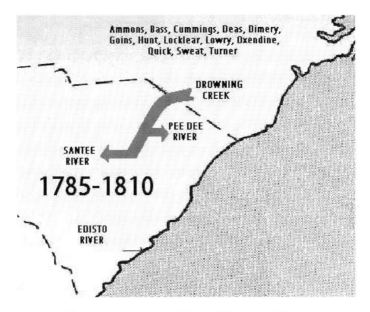

Figure 4: Drowning Creek Migratory Wave

wards the end of the 1800's.

The neighbors of these Indian people seem to have developed a mental disconnect between the romanticized image of the Western Plains Indian and the reality of the brown-skinned people who lived just down the road. A result of this disconnect was the creation of illogical "nick-names" for their darker pigmented citizens; names like "Red Bones," "Brass Ankles," "Croatans" and "Turks." Even these derisive labels did not appear to dilute the Indians' own self-identity evidenced by one non-Indian's statement. "They claim to be Indians," she said on the sly "but they're not real Indians."

Strangely, it wasn't any sense of ancestral pride or unwillingness to assimilate on the part of the Indians that allowed them to maintain their distinctively separate communities even into the modern era, it was the unwillingness of the White "power structure" to accept them as social equals and/or accord them equal legal status. Given the chance, Indians of the Carolinas would have enthusiastically molded themselves into mirror images of their White neighbors much like the 5 civilized tribes attempted to do. In the few instances where South Carolina Indians were able to gain legal concessions as to their Whiteness, they were more than happy to accept it. The overbearing pressure of Jim Crow society would not allow for the Indian ideal of social equality, however, and Indians were left only with a Herculean struggle to not be reduced to the social status of the Negro. This constant desperation fostered a virulent anti-Negro racism among the Carolina Indians, a social disease that is still rampant among the older community members.

POW—WOW FOR CHIEFS—Three South Carolina Indian chiefs were among a gathering of several tribes near Holly Hill recently. From left, are: Hutson Crummie, Santee tribe, Holly Hill; Homer Campbell, Pee Dee tribe, Dillon; and Leon Muckenfuss, Edisto tribe, Ridgeville. The tribes are reportedly seeking "first class status" as citizens of the Palmetto State. (Staff photo)

Indians Meet Near Holly Hill, Map Plans To Improve Status

Representatives of the Santee, Edisto, Pee Dee, and Lumbee Indians met recently in the White Oak community near Holly Hill to map plans for improving their status as first class citizens in South Carolina.

Helen Amerson, secretary, and Louise Branham, a counselor for the Edisto and Santee tribes, said the Indians are tired of their second class status and listed two priorities for action: getting federal and state recognition for the native Americans of the Palmetto State, and getting Indian people registered to vote.

Four members of various tribes were invited to speak to the S. C. Lutheran Synod in convention at Newberry last month. There they presented the same two priorities.

A representative of the synod's Social Ministry Committee pointed out after the meeting in Newberry that under the state constitution, "South Carolina recognizes only whites, blacks, and others."

Mrs. Amerson said the Santee group near Holly Hill and the Edisto tribe of the Four Holes Swamp area were working closely together now to improve their educational levels and life styles.

"We have 20 persons enrolled in adult education classes at White Oak," Mrs. Amerson said, "and a qualified teacher to help these people reach their goals."

The education program is reportedly funded by the Coastal Plains Development Corporation with Title 6 funds from the governor's Manpower program.

Grace Lowry of the Lumbee tribe, one of the speakers addressing the Lutherans at Newberry, was among the Indian women in attendance at the Holly Hill meeting.

Figure 5: Indians Meet Near Holly Hill (Newspaper)

At mid-century an academic interest in the "remnant

Indian" communities of the Southeast came into vogue. It was during this era that the phrase "tri-racial isolates" was coined, a phrase that subsequent researchers, and the Indian people themselves, have worked hard to antiquate. Scholars such as Frank Speck, Brewton Berry, and Robert Thomas spent countless hours of fieldwork among the Indians of both South and North Carolina and their writings reflect the racial pre-conceptions and attitudes of both the White citizenry and their Indian neighbors. Speck, Berry, Thomas, Mooney, and other experts in the field all came to a consensus that there were seven clearly distinct Indian communities in South Carolina. Referring to them by their contrived labels they identified the Wassamasaw, Edisto, Santee, and Beaver Creek Indians all of which they grouped under the name "Brass Ankles," the Cheraws of Sumter under the name "Red Bones" and later as "Turks," the Pee Dee as "Croatans," and the Waccamaw as "Dimerys." These same experts surmised that these fanciful labels were meant to imply Indian ancestry among those they referred to, all the while making note as to the polar opposite ancestry claims of the Whites and the Indians themselves.

While the White southerners were riding a racial purity high horse through sleepy Carolina towns trumpeting the tri-racial origins of those brown-skinned people who lived on the out-skirts, the Indians were hitching a wagon to that horse equally loudly proclaiming their strictly bi-racial ancestry. While the Indians and Whites mutually agreed as to the White and Indian mixture in their blood, it was the question of Negro ancestry that invariably fueled the racial debate. This popular notion of Negro ancestry, a legacy of the "one-drop rule," gave the Carolina White community the social toolbox necessary to construct, and maintain, the status quo. Sometimes they would pull their "Negro blood" scalpel to delicately maneuver the Indians into a "third race" tier, socially somewhere between Whites and Blacks. Other times they would pull their "Negro blood" mallet to pound the Indians "back into their place."

At no time was this social tool used more than when local

Indian men, returning from service in World War Two with a new-found world view and sense of pride, began demanding better education for their children. Not satisfied to just improve the conditions of their small "special" schools the State had provided, the Indians began demanding that their children attend school alongside local White children. The era of school integration spewed a wealth of documentation on the origins of these "mysterious" Indians as the schools tried desperately to maintain their lily-White status and the Indians to document their Native roots. In the end it was the Indians who won the battle. The public schools grudgingly enrolled the Indian children, while the "special" schools quietly closed their doors. Sadly, in regards to maintaining their insulated communities and blood quantum, winning this battle appears to have heralded the Indians losing the war. A common lament among the current Indian leaders and elders is to bemoan the dilution of their community to out-marriage and the decline of their population as better educated youth move to areas such as Columbia, Fayetteville, Savannah, and even Florida.

"Gone to Florida" is a phrase heard in every small Indian hamlet throughout South Carolina. Historical economic opportunities such as the timber boom of the 1800's and the citrus industry of the 1950's lured Indian men and their families in droves to the Sunshine State. Most returned, but some stayed to form their own communities. Even now, it appears these same economic conditions continue to fuel these migrations to the Gulf Coast as almost every Indian you meet in South Carolina has a sibling, cousin, or child that lives in Florida.

One striking phenomenon of Indian affairs in the Palmetto State is that that the tribes appear to be following a timeline twenty years behind the rest of Indian Country. The pan-Indianism and political activism that swept the western reservations in the 60's is mirrored by similar events in South Carolina's 1980's. The governmental negotiations, legal haranguing, and economic adventurism of Indian Country's 80's are just now being explored by South Carolina's tribes. In the mid-1980's Indian leaders Gilbert Blue (Catawba), James Caulder (Pee Dee), Matthew Creel (Edisto), and Henry Platt (Santee) succeeded in securing the establishment of the Palmetto Indian Affairs Commission. The PIAC, at its inception, was conceived to be a vehicle by which elected officials and the various tribes could establish a government-to-government relationship. In reality, the absence of knowledge about modern Indian Country and the unique social needs and legal rights of Indian people by the South Carolina government and also the lack of political sophistication on the part of the tribal representatives caused the PIAC to grind to an ineffective halt. South Carolina eventually rescinded the authority, and in effect the existence, of the PIAC. Only recently, in the early 21st Century, have the tribes been able to rekindle a delicate spark of political dialogue.

Figure 6: A representative of the Governor's Office reads a proclamation establishing a "Native American Day" as Chief Hatcher (Waccamaw) looks on.

In 2004 South Carolina passed legislation instituting a system by which Tribes could become "recognized." Legislators gave the South Carolina Commission for Minority Affairs au-

thority over the Tribal recognition process, a position the SC-
CMA was arguably neither prepared nor qualified to oversee.
Some years have passed since the enactment of the "recognition legislation," and several tribes have been able to successfully navigate the recognition criteria—criteria whose fluid in-
terpretations seem to change from year-to-year and committee
member-to-member. A few tribal groups, previously unheard of
and certainly not mentioned by such knowledgeable academia
as Speck and Berry, have been able to gain State recognition
during the SCCMA's early handling of the process. Others, including some of these same Indian people identified by Speck
and Berry in the 1900's as clearly distinct Indian communities,
have been unable to conquer the political hurdles inherent in the
recognition process.

Much work remains for the leaders of the Tribal communities as they suffer from the same economic, educational, cultural, and health woes as the rest of Indian Country. Whether
they will manipulate this latest wave of activism to cement their
position in the Palmetto State's political landscape, or remain
strangers in their own land remains to be seen.

Figure 7: Santee Gate

Chapter 1

The Wassamasaw

South Carolina's low country is a region dotted by murky swamps, lily-pad-choked ponds, and acres of barren timber cuts. It is a district defined by the Edisto River, which cuts through its heart.

Several small Indian communities have lived in this region for well over 200 years. The most eastern of these groups is the Wassamasaw (a Muskogee word meaning "good water") or Varnertown Indians, located at the border of the Goose Creek city limits halfway between Summerville and Moncks Corner.

Traveling north on US17A one would first observe a white and black historical marker on the eastern shoulder of the highway planted near the driveway of a machine shop. Placed here in October of 2007, the sign outlines the existence, and origins of a "distinct Native American community."[1] Benjamin Drive, a thin clay road next to the machine shop, serves as the virtual backbone of the present-day Wassamasaw community. The Varner surname adorns almost every mailbox on both sides of Benjamin Drive's L-shaped length.

About mid way down the drive is a fresh slab of concrete where Mike Rochay, son of Pearl Varner, is building his new home. "I've lived all over this White man's world and I just

---

[1]Written on the reverse side of the sign shown on the next page.

never felt right," says Rochay in between the percussive thumps
of his nail gun. "I'm moving back so that I can get back into
my heritage. It's for the community, that's what it's all about."
Rochay can easily recount how his new home will sit where his
family's crop field used to be, however the Wassamasaw Indian
tenure on this land goes back much further.

Figure 1.1: Historical marker on US17A

Between 1800 and 1820 census schedules reflect the Indian
family surnames of Williams, Varner, Clark and Broad living on
the outskirts of the Saint James Goose Creek District. William
Williams and his wife Rebecca, mentioned specifically as core
ancestors by the Wassamasaw, can be found on the 1850 to 1880
Goose Creek Parish census schedules. Both were consistently
recorded as non-White. Looking further back in the same area
one will find Williams' father, also named William Williams,
who was born circa 1750. This elder Williams was most likely
the same "Billey Williams" who drew Revolutionary War ser-

vice pay under Captain Drennan's Catawba Indian unit. Now this is certainly not a definitive testament to Williams being a Catawba, as many other smaller tribes had previously joined ranks with the Catawba including the Waxhaw, Pee Dee, Congaree, Cheraw, Wateree, and others.

The official Wassamasaw historical account begins with the marriage of William Varner to Mary Williams, some time around 1878. However, eighteen years earlier records identify an already cohesive community comprised of the Indian surnames of Driggers, Mitchum, Williams, Locklear, Veno, and Varner. Ten years later the same community consisted of the same Williams, Locklear, and Varner families but now joined by Dangerfield and Platt individuals. These two latter surnames would later become associated with the Santee Indians near Holly Hill.

Figure 1.2: Geneva Varner Clark family, 1938

As the nineteenth Century closed, the Williams and Locklear surnames diminished among the Wassamasaw Indians while the prolific Varners became a surname synonymous with

Indian ancestry in the area. So much so, that the community became known as "Varnertown."

Figure 1.3: Mike Rochay (Wassamasaw) building his new home on Benjamin Drive, 2009

Before desegregation, the children of Varnertown attended at least five Indian schools in the area. These included the Barrows Mission School, Pine Ridge School, the Red School (a part of St. Barnabas Mission), Pine View School, and Varner Indian School. The Varnertown Indian youth were served by these "special" schools consistently from 1887 to 1963 when the Varner Indian School was closed and the children integrated into public schools. All of the small, wooden Indian schools have long since been demolished and now are only evidenced by the memory of the older tribal members.

The Wassamasaw Tribe of Varnertown Indian People took quick action when the State of South Carolina instituted recognition procedures, and the Tribe was approved for recognition in 2005. Since gaining that recognition much has not changed for the individual tribal members. They still sit on the porches of their trailers and wood frame houses waving to family members passing on the short dirt road. They still bury their people at old Williams Cemetery, which still has graves discernible by the ancient Indian tradition of conch-shell markers. They have monthly meetings at a small home on Benjamin Drive where they discuss family, neighborhood, and tribal matters.

Given their density in a small community, and strong identity, the Varnertown Indians will not likely lose their separate identity for many generations yet, if ever. More likely, with sufficient social support on the part of the state, and under the guidance of an energetic and intelligent tribal council, the Wassamasaw will have a bright future.

Figure 1.4: Wassamasaw tribal member, 2009

Chapter 2

The Edisto

The Edisto River, a deep and shadowy waterway winds its way through the heart of the low country swamps making its way from near Columbia to Charleston. It is a sometimes-treacherous stream and does not give up its mysteries easily. Equally mysterious has been the history of the Four Holes Edisto tribe, which resides on both banks of the river from which they took their name. On the Edisto's swampy south bank, at the junction of highways 61 and 651, is the hamlet formerly known as "Creeltown," which still supports a church, cemetery, and small store. Crossing the river on Givhan's Ferry Road and traveling about five miles northeast towards Ridgeville one will encounter the Four Holes Edisto Indian Community Center.

The community center is a well-kept block building that sits at the heart of a dense Indian community known as "Four Holes." Under the energetic leadership of Chief Anthony Davidson and Vice Chief Andy Spell the community center remains a whirlwind of activity as the tribe organizes pow-wows, cultural training courses, and elder services programs. While the Edisto tribal government strives to fulfill the Indians' physical needs, the Four Holes Church satisfies the spirit. Churches and Indian schools have stood at both Four Holes and Creeltown from the 1880's onward, but the Indians have resided on these same plots of land since at least a century earlier.

Figure 2.1: Vice-Chief Andy Spell (Edisto) and Chief Anthony Davidson (Edisto), 2009

Several notable researchers, making inquiry into the history of this tribe, have stated that the ancestors of the Edisto are not documented from 1750 to 1830 as "they disappear from the census entirely because, as the record states, Indians pay no taxes."[1] A careful study of the early census schedules, however, reveals that the Edisto ancestors were indeed recorded. As early as 1790 one can find Sally Buck, John Winningham, Lewis Winningham (Winningham, Windham, and Windom are used interchangeably on the schedules and will be written here as they were recorded), and William Creel all reported as "Free Persons of Color" and living in the general area of present-day Creeltown. It has also been suggested that the Edisto surnames of Muck-

---

[1] Wes White, "Some of the Written Memory of the Natchez-Kusso Indians of Edisto River," 1980 pamphlet.

enfuss and Muckelvaney are of Indian origin. These names do sound unique in their present spelling and pronunciation; however both surnames were those of early White Colleton County settlers, namely Thomas McInfuss and John McKlevaney.

By 1810 the Indian hamlet on the south bank of the Edisto was inhabited by "other free persons" Lewis Winnington, John Winningham, Sam Patrick, Right Patrick, and Jeremiah Patrick. These Patricks were descendants of Ezekiel Patrick, recorded as a "Free Person of Color" in the 1790 Dillon County area. Living here also was the White family of Thomas McInfuss.

Figure 2.2: Preston Davidson (Edisto), 1984

The 1850 census schedule reflects that two interconnected

communities had evolved on opposite banks of the Edisto. To the south lived Charles Patrick, Nancy Windham, Elijah Patrick, Sylvester Windham, Henry Johnson and his wife Margaret Patrick, and the families of Daniel Miller and Thomas Muckenfusshere listed as "White." On the north bank, near Four Holes Swamp, lived Eleanor Thomly, Mary Redmon, George Hood, Zachariah Gordon, Nehemiah Jones, George and Isaac Davidson, Ann Patrick, James Jones, and Charity Gordon.

Ten years later the southerly hamlet had expanded while Four Holes had lost the majority of its inhabitants. The Indian families of Isaac Winningham, J. Bunch and grandson Tobias Winningham, Henry Johnson, John Dunn, Gordon Jackson (of the same Jackson family who would later join the Santee Indians), and Margaret Creel were living south of Edisto along with the "White" families of William Miller and Thomas Muckenfuss. George Muckenfuss, son of Thomas, had recently married the daughter of Indian John Dunn, and this appears to have been the beginning of the "non-White" Muckenfuss lineage. At this same time period the only Indian family recorded at Four Holes was that of Isaac Davidson and his wife Sophronia Windham, here listed as "White."

From the Civil War to the turn of the twentieth century there was an observable strengthening of both the Creeltown and Four Holes settlements. Indians such as Henry Creel, John Creel, Nancy Spell, and George Davidson were raising large families at Creeltown while Adeline Spell, Mary Jones, Isaac Davidson, John Platt, and Sylvester Windom were doing the same at Four Holes.

Around 1900 the families of John and Sam Muckelvaney settled into the Four Holes community. These two brothers were sons of Samuel Mackalvany, a timber rafter working on the Little Salkehatchie River near Bell's Crossroads. Samuel, in turn, was the son of John McKlevany of Orangeburg and his "other free person" wife.

When the First World War broke out all the of-age Creel,

Figure 2.3: Four Holes Indian School, circa 1980

Davidson, Mackelvaney, and Davidson men were recorded on the civil enlistments of 1917. While the Davidson, Mackelvaney, and Muckenfuss men were haphazardly recorded as different races, or the race section left blank, the Creels were uniformly identified being at least half Indian.

With the arrival of desegregation, the Indian School at Creeltown closed in 1966 while the school at Four Holes hung on for another three years. While integration was meant to level the educational playing field, the Edisto Indian families began to notice a systematic effort by Ridgeville School officials to disenfranchise their youth. Edisto children were denied the same books and supplies as their White counterparts, segregated to un-maintained classrooms, or simply ignored by their teachers. As a result many Indian parents ceased sending their children to Ridgeville. Since the Creeltown and Four Holes schools were no longer funded, this left the Indian children with no educational outlet.

Luckily, social workers took notice, temporary funding was acquired, and the "Four Holes Freedom School" opened in the old Indian schoolhouse. Activists were soon able to negotiate

Figure 2.4: Edisto Indian Community Center, 2009

the reentry of the children into Ridgeville, and the Four Holes School once again shut its doors in 1970. On a positive note, this gave the Edisto Indians the dubious distinction of having had "the last Indian school in South Carolina," which remains a source of pride for them today. The Roman Catholic Church also conducted extensive social work within the Edisto Indian community during this era, and the nuns Sister Carol and Sister Mary are especially remembered fondly by the Indians.

The Edisto Indians have been politically active in Indian affairs since at least the 1950s and this remains true today. They officially incorporated under the name of Four Holes Indian Organization, Inc. and under former Chiefs Preston Davidson, Eddie Martin, and Matthew Creel they were a major player in the formation of the Palmetto Indian Affairs Commission. The Edisto have a pending application for federal recognition with the Bureau of Indian Affairs but a "difference of opinion" has stalled any application for state recognition. The Edisto believe that state recognition was granted to them pursuant to an earlier Legislative resolution in 1984, however the South Carolina Commission for Minority Affairs disagrees. With or without state recognition the Edisto have been successful in strengthen-

Figure 2.5: Edisto Indians preparing for annual pow-wow, 2009

ing their community through acquiring grants regularly, numerous cultural activities, and maintaining a highly visible community center that serves as a daily reminder of Edisto Indian identity.

Figure 2.6: Four Holes Highway Sign

Chapter 3

The Santee

Driving northwest on Highway 176 the traveler will observe the thick forest and swamps of the low country begin to thin out, replaced by long stretches of cleared fields and weathered farm houses bordered by wooded creek bottoms. This is terrain that characterizes most of South Carolina. Entering downtown Holly Hill, taking a right on Eutaw Road and traveling north, one would reach Indian Town Lane at a hard left-hand turn in the road. This is the territory of the Santee Indians. Much like the relationship between the Wassamasaw and Benjamin Drive, Bayview Drive defines the Santee. Bayview is a curvy stretch of blacktop that winds its way past farm fields, modern homes, trailers, the old White Oak Church and School, and the tribal office of the Santee Indians.

Just north of the tribal office lives Chief Roosevelt Scott, a man who doesn't agree with the stereotypical headdress adorned Indian chief. "I don't feel the need for the feathers and beads." Scott says, "I don't need it and my people don't need it." At least one tribal member agrees. Desiré Platt, a Santee Indian councilwoman who also lives on Bayview says, "There's so much work to be done. We need more workers." The need for Santee "workers" appears genuine as the tribe has lost a significant portion of their population to Florida migrations, and even more

have moved to other areas leaving behind their historic community. "We need State and Federal recognition to bring our people
back," says Scott. If Scott succeeds these Indians will be returning to a community their tribe has inhabited for over 250 years.

Figure 3.1: Indian Town Lane Street Sign

One of the earliest known ancestors of the Santee is John
Scott, an Indian who purchased 200 acres near Holly Hill from
fellow Indian John Chavis in 1753. John and his brother, James
Scott (an ancestor of the Sumter Cheraw) were both enlisted by
Charleston officials to serve as interpreters for visiting Catawba
Indians. There is good evidence that both John and James
originally carried the surname "Busby" but, for reasons lost to
history, assumed the Scott name. Just before the Civil War a
group of Indian families with the surnames Jackson, Russell,
Sweat, and Weatherford moved en mass from the Mount Holly
area to the Holly Hill outskirts. The Sweats among the Santee
are lineal descendants of Daniel, the son of Ephraim Sweat.
Ephraim was one of the Indians included on the 1773 "list of the
mob raitously <sic> assembled together in Bladen County."[1]
Ephraim's brother, William, founded the Sweat surname among

---

[1] From a letter by Archibald McKissack, Bladen County Justice of the

those Indians now known as Lumbees. Ephraim, after living near John Scott for several decades, moved on to Opelousas, Louisiana where he founded the Sweat surname among the people known as "Red Bones."

Figure 3.2: Santee Indian Tribe Road Sign

By the beginning of the 1900's the Indians north of Holly Hill had founded the White Oak Church and School and had attracted other Indian families including the Dangerfields, Mitchums, Platts, and Weatherfords who had moved in from areas closer to Charleston. The World War One civil enlistments of 1917 recorded nearly twenty males living north of Holly Hill as "Indian," and all carried the surnames of Jackson, Mitchum, Platt, Russell, Scott, Sweat, or Weatherford. Finally the 1930 census schedule of Holly Hill Township reflects twelve Indian households living north of town, these also bearing the Santee Indian surnames.

White Oak Indian School was closed and its children integrated into public schools in the 60's without too much excitement, however this was not the case in regard to at least one Santee family who had moved to Florida.

Allen Platt and his wife Laura Dangerfield had moved to

Peace, to the governor of North Carolina titled, "A list of the rogues: a list of the mob raitously assembled together in Bladen County, October 13th 1773."

Figure 3.3: Family of Allen Platt and Laura Dangerfield, 1955

Lake County, Florida and enrolled their children into a local White school. Enraged White parents, with the aid of the local sheriff, protested and succeeded in having the Platt children barred from school.

The Platts enlisted legal aid and this began Allen Platt et al v. Board of Public Instruction of Lake County, Florida. The Florida court performed extensive investigation into the Platts' ancestry and social standing in the Holly Hill, SC area. For the most part, the court discovered that the families who lived along Bayview were generally regarded as being of Indian-White admixture and there were even some records calling the Platts "Croatan Indians." The Lake County court ruled in favor of the Platt children and they resumed school attendance.

More recently the Santee tribe was instrumental in the formation of the Palmetto Indian Affairs Commission and acquired a state grant to purchase ten acres of land on which now stands the Santee tribal office. They successfully gained state recognition in 2005 and have a pending application for Federal recognition by the Bureau of Indian Affairs.

Winning small political battles, however, has done little to alleviate the social woes of the Santee Indians. Suffering from a lack of funds and dwindling tribal population, one can only hope that Chief Scott has some tricks up his sleeve to "bring our people back."

Figure 3.4: Chief Roosevelt Scott (Santee), 2009

Chapter 4

The Beaver Creek

About halfway between the home of the Edisto Tribe and Columbia, in the very heart of South Carolina's sleepy agriculture district of Orangeburg County, lies an area claimed as the historical homeland of the Beaver Creek Indians. Here the Edisto River forks into two branches forming a northern and southern border for such small towns as Neeses, Livingston, and North. The Beaver Creek, a collection of scattered Indian families have had ancestors in this same "fork of the Edisto" for nearly 225 years.

During the chaos of the Revolutionary War many Indian men enlisted, but not before moving their families north to the relative safety of the North Carolina interior. After the close of the War the fledgling American government began issuing its own land patents, numerous Indian men claimed plots near their old home places, and quickly moved their families back south.

The Braveboy, Chavis, Hollman, and Williams families were just such Indian settlers. Lewis Braveboy, Elijah Chavis, Mary Chavis, and Richard Chavis all filed patents for land in an area called "Cracker's Neck" near Rocky Swamp in present-day Orangeburg County in mid-1784. All of the aforementioned Indian families migrated down from the Indian settlement on Fishing Creek, Granville County, North Carolina with a brief, one or two decade stay in the Drowning Creek area. Lewis Braveboy's father, Joshua Braveboy, left several sons among the Drowning Creek "Lumbee" as well as founded the Braveboy surname among the "Pee Dee" of Marlboro-Dillon. Eighteen years later Lazarus Chavis filed his land plat "in the fork of the Edisto" near Rocky Swamp, and this is the ancestor that the majority of the modern Beaver Creek Indians claim.

Figure 4.1: Beaver Creek Tribal Office Sign

The 1790 census schedule reflects Lewis Braveboy, Elijah Chavis, Lazarus Chavis, Abraham Hollman, Abraham Scott, William Scott, Abraham Williams, Amy Williams, and Joseph Williams as families of "Free Persons of Color." These identical families can be found in the 1800 to 1840 time period residing in the same Orangeburg County area and recorded alternately as "Other Free Persons" and "Free White." After 1850 the family names of Gleaton, Hoffman, and Hutto would also become synonymous with Indian ancestry as White men by those names intermarried with the Chavis and Williams families.

In December of 1859 a son of Lazarus Chavis, Frederick Chavis who had moved to nearby Edgefield County, filed a petition to the South Carolina Legislature on behalf of himself and several other Indians of the county. The petition was an inquiry, "If persons of Indian descent are considered to be free persons of color and liable for the poll tax." Other persons that Frederick filed on behalf of were his son Lewis Chavis, his daughter Durany Chavis, Jehu Jones, Bartley Jones, Mary Jones, Jonathan Williams, and Polly Dunn.

Figure 4.2: Chief Louie Chavis (Beaver Creek), 2009

In 1860 the census schedule shows John Williams, Abraham Chavis, Nancy Chavis, James Hutto, Josiah Chavis, Phillip Chavis, and John Scott all living in a close community at the edge of Bull Swamp in Orangeburg, and all recorded as "mulatto." This is one of the few times in all the available census schedules that members of this community are recorded as any other than "White."

Between 1880 and 1900 a church was founded near Rocky Swamp called "Rocky Swamp United Methodist." This church closed at some point, but was reopened in 2001. This church has, as it did in the past, a predominantly Indian congregation. The Four Pines School for Indians was also founded nearby and this is where the Chavis, Gleaton, Hollman, Hutto, Williams, and other Indian children attended school until the desegregation era of the 1960's after which they attended Orangeburg.

Figure 4.3: Harold Hollman (Beaver Creek), 2009

At the time of the 1917 civil enlistments for World War One at least two Orangeburg residents were recorded as "Indian," these being Riley Chavis and Jerry Bunch. Around this same time period the term "Croatan" began appearing on the Beaver Creek Indian birth and death certificates. Although these Indians had little or no contact with their distant cousins in Robeson County who were then officially called the "Croatan tribe," perhaps the large number of Chavises among the Robeson Indians influenced the Orangeburg officials to also use this designation. Given that the Beaver Creek Indians were also known by the derisive slurs "Brass Ankles" and "Red Legs," it would appear that "Croatan" might have been the lesser of two evils. After the end of the Civil War the Indian families of the "fork of the Edisto" multiplied and spread out on individual farm plots across Orangeburg and neighboring counties, and this remains true of the present membership of the Beaver Creek tribe. While members are spread from Columbia to Charleston, they have a centralized tribal headquarters in the town of Salley where they have regular tribal meetings, homecoming dinners, and pow-wows.

The Orangeburg area Indians officially organized under the name "Beaver Creek" in the late 1990's and were able to attain state recognition in August of 2006 under the leadership of Chief Louie Chavis and Vice-Chief Kenneth Adams. Those same leaders hope to take the next step and attain Federal recognition; a move Chavis and Adams hope will draw their members back closer to their roots and proud heritage.

Chapter 5

The Cheraw

Leaving the low country and driving north on I-95, it's a short drive to Sumter County. Exiting the interstate on highway 378, driving east and bypassing the city of Sumter, the traveler will soon reach the borders of Shaw Air Force Base. Here also one will encounter terrain unique in all of South Carolina as the familiar flat farm fields are replaced by almost mountainous, forested hills. This area came to be known as the High Hills of Santee. This is the historic territory of a large Indian-blooded populace formerly known by the derisive slur "Turks."

Though known by the name "Turks" since at least 1913, the swarthy, clannish people were no more realistically "Turks" than the Indian tribes detailed in previous chapters were "Brass Ankles." These copper-skinned, high cheek-boned people whose grandparents learned that they could gain equality under the identity of "Turks" that they were denied as "Indians," have in the most recent generation begun to reclaim their rightful birthright as persons of Indian descent.

The core ancestors of the Cheraw Indians were 6 men who arrived in the area of High Hills circa 1804. This arrival date can be documented through comparing the birth dates and birthplaces on older census schedules. Prior to 1804, four of the men were living in the "Charraw Settlement" of Indians living along

Drowning Creek in present-day Robeson County, North Carolina.

These four men were John Scott, Aaron Oxendine who married a daughter of Scott, William Deas, and John Chavis. Aaron Oxendine's father, Charles, was the ancestor of all of the Oxendines among the Lumbee Indians today, Cudworth and Charles, Aaron's uncle and brother respectively, founded the surname among the Pee Dee Indians of Marlboro and Dillon. William Deas was the son of Moses, who also seeded the surname among the present-day Lumbee. John Chavis was the son of Ishmael, and the nephew of Lazarus Chavis, the ancestor of the Beaver Creek Indians.

Figure 5.1: Cheraw tribal members, 2009

The remaining two men were John Buckner who married Sarah Jane Oxendine, and Joseph Benenhaley, a "Caucasian of Arab descent." John Buckner was described by one elderly resident of Sumter as "to be almost pure Indian," In addition Aaron

Oxendine, John Scott, and Ishmael Chavis appear on a list of "heads of Indian families" in 1790 Robeson County compiled by C.D. Brewington in 1959. As time progressed, the Indians of Sumter formed two communities, the Chavis, Gibbs, Goins, and Smilings near Privateer Township and the Benenhaleys, Buckners, Deas, Oxendines, and Scotts near Dalzell. Though the two hamlets were separated by about ten miles the community members maintained social connections as several members of the Dalzell settlement appear on the records of the Bethesda Church at Privateer, the opposite is true in the records of the High Hills and Long Branch churches at Dalzell, and several children from Privateer attended school at the Dalzell school. Both of these small communities were called "Red Bones" by their White neighbors, however the Chavis, Goins, and Smilings of Privateer eventually moved back to Robeson circa 1910 and the people at Dalzell began to be called "Turks" by their neighbors.

These swarthy, secretive High Hills natives were thrust upon the national scene in the 1950's when the ACLU took part in their legal action to force Shaw Heights School to accept their children. The legal case also piqued the interest of a few amateur historians who, after performing some shallow research, printed imaginative histories of these "Turks;" histories which have caused a veritable identity crisis among the brown-skinned people of Sumter.

Following the legal case Brewton Berry, Ira Kaye, and Anne Gregorie wrote numerous accounts about the history of the Sumter Indian people. In an attempt to explain their historical origins, all three mistakenly quoted the 1791 petition of "Free Moors; Subjects of the Emperor of Morocco" as if it had some connection to the Sumter Indians. The 1791 petition was filed on behalf of two families residing in Charleston, and besides, a later petition was filed specifically on behalf of the Sumter Indians.

A serious search of Sumter's records would have rewarded any of these researchers with the 1858 "Resolution Imposing

Figure 5.2: Jessie Lee Benenhaley (Cheraw), 2009

Capitation Tax on Egyptians and Indians as now on Free Blacks, Mulattoes, and Mestizos," a resolution filed on behalf of the Benenhaley family, described as "Egyptian," and the Chavis, Deas, Goins, Oxendine, and Scott families, described as "Indian."

All three researchers agreed that Aaron Oxendine was an Indian connected to the "Lumbees," yet also blindly quoted the fantastical origin theory presented by Thomas Sumter III (Great-grandson of the famous Revolutionary War General Thomas Sumter) in his book "Stateburg and its People." Thomas wrote that General Sumter, scouting for men at the onset of the Revolutionary War, stopped at Goose Creek near Charleston and enlisted an Arab named Yusef Ben Ali (alias Joseph Benenhaley) as a scout and a part-French man who had changed his name to Scott as his bugler.

An earlier letter, written by Thomas' father calls into question this account. In 1889 Sebastian D'Amblemont Sumter, the son of General Sumter's only child, wrote "As to the original Benenhaley, I know nothing having seen him only once or twice in my early boyhood nearly sixty years ago. I am very certain that General Sumter had no hand in his importation and do not think he made his appearance here until after the first decade of the present century." Since Sebastian admitted to knowing noth-

Figure 5.3: Jan Lewandowski (Cheraw), 2009

ing about the ancestry of the brown-skinned people near Dalzell in 1889, it's a wonder why his son Thomas would claim to know so much forty years later, or why such reputable scholars would choose to quote a book which was simply repeating local legend and rumor with no first-hand facts.

Several descendants of Joseph Benenhaley have taken DNA tests which returned with distant Arabic results, so this appears to lend credence to the legends; however they also returned with a sizeable amount of Native American blood as well, most likely because these same test subjects are also descendants of Indians such as Aaron Oxendine, John Scott, and William Deas. Regardless of where Joseph Benenhaley originated, or what his

"race" was, he was only one man among ten other core ancestors who have undeniable documentation of Indian ancestry.
"He was only one man," a Cheraw tribal council member said,
"and one man does not make a bloodline."

Besides their ancestors having migrated from an Indian
community of "Charraw," numerous more current accounts of
their Indian identity exists. In 1861 seventy-three year old John
Pollard filed an affidavit testifying to the Indian ancestry of the
Scott and Oxendine families. Pollard stated that "the general
striking physiognomial traits of appearance of the Scott family
in general, and relatives, is deeply set with European and Indian
blood."

In 1861 and 1864 Charles Oxendine, the son of Aaron was
listed on the Sumter tax rolls as "Indian," and between World
Wars One and Two, William Chavis, Altimont Chavis, Jim Goings, John Smiling, and Roy Oxendine were all enlisted as "Indian" men. Hamilton McMillan of Fayetteville in 1890 wrote a
letter to the Commissioner of Indian Affairs in Washington regarding the Indians of Robeson County and he stated that "In
Sumter County, South Carolina, there is a branch of the tribe."
A letter from the Secretary of the Interior in 1914 entitled "A
Report on the Condition and Tribal Rights of the Indians of
Robeson and Adjoining Counties" repeats the theory that the
people of Sumter were a branch of the Robeson Indians and further stated that, at one time, the Robeson Indians "were known
as 'Red Bones'...they are known by this name in Sumter County,
South Carolina."

In 1939, the authorities of Jackson County, Florida sent a
letter to Mister J.R. Lowrey of the Cherokee Normal School in
Pembroke, questioning a Sumter Indian connection to a community in Florida. (This will be discussed later in this chapter.)
The letter mentions that the School Superintendent of Sumter
revealed, "indeed the names of Scott and Goings are known to
him and that they are generally believed in that County to be of
Indian blood." The Sumter Superintendent also wrote, "a school
was maintained for the Indian race in that County," and he re-

Figure 5.4: Oxendine family (Cheraw), 2009

ferred to a Mr. Benenholy as "an old Indian of that County."

A 1949 newspaper article entitled "'Turks' Seeking Educational Opportunities for Children" reported the Sumter people's appearance as "Many of them look like American Indians," and stated that "Professor Harry H. Turney-High, an anthropologist on the faculty of the University of South Carolina, says that there is a strong physical similarity between the purer strains of Turks and a number of American Indian types."

F. Kinloch Bull, born 1896, wrote in his memoir "Random Recollections of a Long Life" that the Sumter Indians generally had "Straight black hair and copper colored complexion." Bull remembered that in the early 1900's the undisputed "Chief" was "an old veteran called Tom Turk, but I do not remember ever hearing his real name." Old Tom "exerted almost supreme authority" over the people of the community and even controlled their votes.

The elderly Bull singled out one family whose eldest member, John Buckner, "appeared to be almost pure Indian." Bull remembered the name "Redbone" but it had fell out of use when

Figure 5.5: Dalzell School for "Turks" circa 1954, the school
closed in 1961

the Privateer Indian settlement relocated back to Robeson, and
the term was replaced with "Turk." Finally, in 1963, Muhit-
tin Guven, a member of the Turkish Parliament, paid a visit to
South Carolina, and upon hearing that there was a community of
"Turks" nearby, paid a visit to Julius Benenhaley, the reported
"King of the clan." The news article reported that Guven did
not recognize the Sumter people as having any of the traits of
Turkish people he was familiar with, and that Julius Benehaley
himself was quoted as saying he didn't know much about the
Turk ancestry but thought that they "had some Indian blood."

Between 1910 and 1913 the Indian families of Chavis,
Goins, and Smilings relocated from Sumter back to Robeson,
North Carolina. When they tried to enroll their children in the
local Indian schools the Trustees of the Indian schools launched
an investigation into their backgrounds. Testimony given
during these hearings is a wealth of information regarding how
the Indian people of Sumter viewed themselves and also how
their White neighbors regarded them. One elderly Goins from
Sumter testified, "our parents went from North Carolina, some
of the older ones, and there were lots of names, Oxendine,
Hunt, Chavis and Goins." L.I. Parrot, the Clerk of the Court
for Sumter County, testified that the brown-skinned people of

Figure 5.6: Hubert "Hub" Scott (Cheraw), Florida, 2004

Sumter "have been known as 'Red Bones' ever since I have been acquainted with the people." Another Indian said "I was raised in Sumter Coun ty...We are Indians in the north, but they gave us the name of 'Red Bones' down there."

An interesting side-story regarding the Sumter Cheraw is the saga of a portion of their tribe that migrated to Florida. Just prior to the onset of the Civil War Absalom Scott, Jacob Scott and Isham Scott left Sumter and journeyed to the "Southern frontier" of northwest Florida. Isham's wife was Margaret Oxendine was conencted to Aaron Oxendine either through blood or marriage. Drawn by the promise of cheap land and bountiful economic opportunities these men purchased property in two sections along the Chipola River and soon started a ferry and mill.

The northernmost settlement, on the headwaters of the Chipola called "Scott Town," was situated on property owned by Absalom Scott and was soon supporting several bountiful farms. The southerly community was on a plot owned by Jacob and Isham Scott and bore a ferry and mill. This hamlet was soon known by the name "Scott's Ferry" as it still is today. In 1860 the Scotts and their relatives were given a special census schedule page where the enumerator wrote a note that claimed the Scotts were "mixed blooded almost white" and that they "live in a settlement or town of their own."

Figure 5.7: Chief Buck Bryant (Cheraw) and Adam Davis (Cheraw), Florida, 1998

In 1862 the Court of Calhoun County, Florida charged Francis "Frank" Hill, the husband of Eliza Scott of Scott's Ferry, with "Fornication wih a Mulatto." Testimony was recorded from several witnesses who testified that they "...knew Isham Scott and Margaret, parents of Eliza, in Sumter, South Carolina. Isham was a man of large amount Indian blood. Margaret was an Oxendine woman of clear complexion nearly white the

Indian still apparent. The grandfather, one Jacob, was said to be a Chief among the Catawba Indians. The Scott family, in general, are regarded as free of negro blood." After presenting this testimony as well as a legal marriage certificate, Frank Hill was found not guilty.

When the Civil War broke out almost all of the able bodied men of the Scott settlements enlisted under the Confederate flag and were physically described as "brown eyes, black hair, dark skin," and several of the older Scotts appeared on Home Guard lists as well. As the War waged on it appears that the Scotts soon developed Union sympathies and those young men who hadn't already been killed in action soon switched sides and enlisted with the Florida Rangers Union force stationed at Apalachicola, Florida. The turning point for the Scott family seems to have been when some Confederate soldiers, either official raiders or deserters, looted the Scott mill and burned it to the ground. While members of the Florida Rangers, these Scott settlement enlistees were described as "half-breed Indians." Fifty years later, when America called her citizens to sign up for World War One civil enlistments, all the of-age men from both Scott Town and Scotts Ferry were recorded as "Indian," "Caucasian-Indian," or "Creole-Indian."

In 1939 a series of written correspondence occurred between Jackson County, Florida, Robeson County, North Carolina, and Sumter County, South Carolina. Mary Scott Porter, a bright and ambitious girl of the Scott Town settlement, had traveled to Pembroke and enrolled in the Cherokee Normal School for Indians. J.R. Lowrey, the Dean of the Normal School, wrote a letter to the Jackson County school officials to inquire whether Mary had attended an "Indian" grade school as she claimed, and whether there was any local knowledge as to her ancestry.

The Jackson County School Superintendent launched an indepth investigation and finally reported, "It is of course possible that they might have a large percentage of Indian blood but I have no information or knowledge as to their ancestry." In the fi-

nal letter of the series the Jackson County Superintendent wrote
the Cherokee Normal School Dean and informed him that, upon
the advice of "Mr. Tom Scott" of the Florida settlement he
had "corresponded with the Superintendent of Sumter County,
South Carolina, the place from which Mr. Scott claimed their
ancestors came." He further wrote "I was informed by him that
indeed the names of Scott and Goings are known to him and that
they are generally believed in that county to be of Indian blood.
He confirmed that a school was maintained for the Indian race
in that county however he was unable to substantiate the church
and family connections that Mr. Scott claims. I am expecting
a return from my letter to Mr. Benenholy, an old Indian of that
county, who should be able to supply more information in that
regard." No response from that "old Indian" Benenhaley has yet
been discovered but it appears Mary Scott Porter was allowed to
continue her schooling.

The "Scott Church," a one room wooden structure built in
1889 that served as a church and school for the Florida Indian
children, still stands today on ten acres owned by the Scott family. This is one of only two Indian schools in all of Florida
outside of the south Florida reservations of the Seminole and
Miccosukee.

The Sumter Cheraw of today are extremely active in the
political and cultural life of South Carolina's Indian people.
Their tribal members attend almost every pow-wow organized
by other South and North Carolina tribes, are integral partici-
pants in the activities of the South Carolina Indian Affairs Committee, and aggressivley pursued state recognition. In December
of 2012 the Palmetto State finally acknowledged the 200 year
presence of the Sumter Band of Cheraw Indians and bestowed
full state recognition to the tribe. The tribal leadership of the
Cheraw plan to turn this victory into real social, economic, and
cultural benefit for their members, and if they continue with the
same vitality and political savy, their future appears bright

Figure 5.8: Elaine Hill (Cheraw), Florida, 2004

Chapter 6

The Pee Dee

Journeying north from the High Hills of Santee one can observe the South Carolina landscape resuming its familiar flat farmland terrain. These same cleared fields interspersed with dilapidated wooden farmhouses, wooded creek bottoms, and occasional impassable swamps continue well beyond the North-South Carolina line. Just south of this line are two counties that border the northern passage of I-95. These are Marlboro County and Dillon County, the historical homeland of the Pee Dee Indians.

The Pee Dee are a tribe whose ancestry, history, and familial relationships are so intertwined with that of the Lumbee tribe that they are virtually the same people; excepting the physical border of a state line and the mental border that the Pee Dee leaders have created to guard their separate identity. Being that their ancestors were establishing homesteads along the Pee Dee River at the same time their siblings were along the Drowning Creek, one could certainly give credence to the Pee Dee tribe's argument that they are a separate people from the Lumbee. "We ain't the same," one Pee Dee leader stated "Some of them came from us, but we didn't come from them."

The earliest U.S. census, that of 1790, reflects that numerous Indian families had already established homesteads in the area of modern Marlboro and Dillon counties. These were the

Figure 6.1: Pee Dee Indians of South Carolina

families of Joshua Braveboy, John and Jordan Chavis, Edmond
Clark, Stewart Cummings, John and Mark Driggers, David
Hatcher, Thomas Jackson, John Turner, and William Sweat.
Both John and Jordan Chavis had been previously taxed for
over a decade in Granville County, North Carolina, before
selling their Granville land in the 1780's. Both brothers along
with their father, Ishmael Chavis, moved briefly down along
the Drowning Creek, but then pushed on south into Marlboro
by the end of the Revolutionary War. Joshua Braveboy, already
an elder by the 1790 census, had been taxed in his homestead
in Bladen County in the 1760's and 1770's before he and
his son Lewis decided to move south. While Joshua stopped
in Marlboro, Lewis continued on to Orangeburg where he is
counted as an ancestor of the Beaver Creek Indians.

    The Braveboy and Clark families had been closely allied
while they were residents of Granville, and this close relationship continued in Marlboro. John and Mark Driggers also were

landowners in the 1760's Bladen area and had sold their North Carolina lands shortly before appearing on the 1790 Marlboro census. Like their parents and/or siblings they had left behind in Robeson, these Indians were recorded as "Free Persons of Color" on the census schedule for that year.

Figure 6.2: Mr. Cummings (Pee Dee) and Chief James Caulder (Pee Dee), 2009

By 1800 the "old Settlers" of Braveboys, Chavises, Clarks, Driggerses, and Turners were joined by a new wave of Indians moving south out of the Drowning Creek area. These included the families of Joshua Ammons, Joseph Bass, John Dimmery, Fanny Hunt, and Charles and Cudworth Oxendine. Both of these Oxendine brothers were sons of Charles Oxendine Senior of Robeson County. Aaron Oxendine, another son of Charles Senior, continued south to settle in Sumter County where he is counted among the ancestors of the Sumter Cheraw. Acquiller Quick also arrived in the Marlboro-Dillon area at this time along with three Locklear brothers who had married three of his daughters. Being that the Indians were living on individually owned plots of land, completely assimilated and acculturated into the southern agricultural lifestyle, and subject to state land and poll taxes, the census enumerator could not record them as "Indians not taxed," and thus they were recorded as "Other Free Persons."

Figure 6.3: Pee Dee Indian Tribe Office Sign

Forty years later the Indian community of Marlboro-Dillon was comprised of virtually the identical families as in 1800. John Ammons, Richard Bass, Sarah Brayboy, John Chavis, Jordan Chavis, Robert Chavis, Hannah Clark, Reubin Clark, Daniel Dimmery, Ann Driggers, Telatha Driggers, Thomas Driggers, Elizabeth Goins, Robert Hale, Lydia Hunt, Thomas Jackson, Thomas Kearsey, George Locklear, Lothlin Locklear, Isham Scott, Margaret Scott, John Turner, Benjamin Quick, Levi Quick, and Malachi Quick were all heads of household here and all recorded this time as either "White" or "Free Colored Persons."

The 1850 census schedule of Marlboro and Marion reflects all of these familiar Indian surnames; names which mirror those occurring in neighboring Robeson. This decade, however, the "Other Free Person" classification is absent and the Indians of the Pee Dee are haphazardly given racial designations as "White," "Mulatto," or "Indian." The 1850 household of Mary Jackson is an excellent example of this arbitrary method of determining race.

Figure 6.4: Chief Tim LaBean (Pee Dee), 2008

Mary Jackson, age 54, was recorded as a "mulatto" head of household, while living with her was her daughter Maria, a 22 year old "Indian." Also in Mary's home were her 84-year-old "Indian" mother-in-law and two "Indian" grandchildren Eliz-

abeth Dimery and John Young. Another example is Robert
Chavis, a 66-year-old "Indian" born in North Carolina, along
with his 44-year-old "White" wife Betsy and three "Mulatto"
children Sara, John, and Jim. Many of the older Indians on this
census schedule also reported North Carolina as their birthplace
including George Locklear, George Lowry, Gilbert Oxendine,
and many others.

Numerous websites and pamphlets regarding the history of
the modern Pee Dee describe a scenario where the Indians "hid
out in swamps to avoid removal" only to reemerge once "desegregation made it safe to be Indian again." This romantic and
stereotypical view of the Pee Dee history is challenged by the
available documentation. From the Civil War to World War Two
there exists a volume of written publications, Court cases, academic studies, and Indian Affairs Office correspondence, which
reveals that the Pee Dee and other Indians of South Carolina
were not "hid out." In fact, the existence and history of these
Indian blooded people were well known both locally and na-
tionally.

An 1890 pamphlet published by historian Hamilton McMillan reported that Indians of the same type as the "Croatans of
Robeson" were living in Sumter, Marlboro, and Dillon counties of South Carolina. The same pamphlet mentioned several
times that the southerly Indians were a "branch of the (Robeson) tribe," but as mentioned before, the modern Pee Dee tribal
leaders hotly contest this.

In 1914 a report was issued from the Secretary of the Interior entitled "A Report on the Condition and Tribal Rights of the
Indians of Robeson and Adjoining Counties of North Carolina."
This report mirrored the conclusions presented by McMillan
over twenty years earlier.

In 1916 James Sprunt, a Civil War veteran and expert on the
history of southeastern North Carolina, published "Chronicles
of the Cape Fear" where he stated that "the Indians living on
the Pee Dee, Santee and their tributaries are the offshoots from
the one tribe or nation, the Cheraw." He also revealed that their

language specifically identified them as one people due to "the termination of names using "aw" as in Waxhaw, Saxapahaw, Cheraw, Waccamaw."

Sprunt's opinion seems to coincide with early records of the Catawba Indians which reflect that when the remnant Pee Dee, Saponi, Congaree, and Waxhaw moved into a unified village on the Catawba reservation, this village was known by the collective name of "Cheraw."

In 1925 Elizabeth Smith conducted a report entitled "An Analysis of a 'Croatan' Community. Smith performed extensive fieldwork in Marlboro County, especially the "northern end...sand hill district." In the report Smith explains that the Marlboro Indians "claim their Indian blood from the Cheraw Indians...that live in and around Roberson County, North Carolina."

These identifications as "Cheraw" should not be perceived as testament that the Indians of Marlboro-Dillon are somehow not descendants of the true Pee Dee tribe. Historical accounts from the colonial period, including those of John Lawson, Governor Spottswood, and Baron Von Graffenried, give convincing evidence that "Cheraw" may have never been a true and independent tribe at all. It appears that "Cheraw," being a corruption of earlier forms like "Saraw" or "Esaw," was simply a Siouan word meaning "the people" and was adopted by early explorers of the Carolinas to describe any of the numerous Siouan-speaking villages. So, in effect the term "Cheraw" was used to identify the Pee Dee, Congaree, Waxhaw, and others much like "Creek" was used to describe the confederated villages of Chattahoochees, Alibamos, Hitchitis, and Yuchis.

In 1878 a church was established for the Indian people in the Red Bluff community. Originally called the "Locklear Church" it became known as the Berea United Methodist. The founding document for the church states that it was founded to serve the spiritual needs of "a long neglected class of people, willing to associate in worships with neither the white people nor the colored people, but prefer to keep to themselves." Though the

Red Bluff church was possibly the oldest in the Marlboro-Dillon area, others existed which had predominantly Indian congregations such as Mount Elem, Pee Dee Chapel, Hickory Grove, Catfish Baptist, and Fairview United Methodist. It is interesting to note that at least two of the Pee Dee Indian churches are members of the Burnt Swamp Baptist Association, an organization founded in 1881 by Lumbee Indian churches.

Figure 6.5: Mount Elem Baptist Church

There were at least two Indian schools for the Pee Dee children, Sardis and Leland Grove. The Sardis Indian School, established in 1895 for Marlboro's children, closed in the 1950's. The Leland Grove Indian School served mainly Dillon children. The Pee Dee were responsible for the groundbreaking legal case which pioneered funding these "special" schools neither as "White" nor "Colored" but as "Indian." In 1913 three Indian children of the Kirby family were dismissed from the Dalcho Public School in Dillon. When a case on behalf of the Kirbys was ruled against by the State Board of Education it was appealed to the State Supreme Court. This Court agreed that funding should be provided by the state for these Indian schools and that funding survived until the early 1970's. Witnesses for the Kirby family testified that they were "Croatan Indians" and members of the Catfish Baptist Church.

Figure 6.6: T.J. Clark (Pee Dee), Rebecca Grooms (Pee Dee), 2008

The Pee Dee Indian Association, Inc. was chartered on November 29th of 1976 and the Pee Dee's have continued to be trailblazers in state Indian affairs as well as the most politically active Indian tribe in South Carolina by far. Pee Dee leaders were a significant force behind the genesis of the Palmetto Indian Affairs Commission of the 1980's. The Pee Dee filed a petition for Federal recognition in January of 1995 which is still pending in the Bureau of Indian Affairs.

A second government representing the Pee Dee, called the Pee Dee Indian Nation of Upper South Carolina, filed a similar petition for Federal recognition in December of 2005. These same "Upper Pee Dee" achieved state recognition in February of 2005, followed closely by the Pee Dee Indian Association in January of 2006. While Chief Caulder of the Pee Dee described achieving state recognition as "a great honor and long awaited acknowledgment by the state that we are who we always said we were," other Pee Dee leaders are not so optimistic. "It's only a piece of paper." Stated Carolyn Chavis-Bolton of the Upper Pee Dee, "Nothing has changed here in 50 years and nothing will." Change will certainly come to the Pee Dee Indians nevertheless, and most likely due to current events regarding their close cousins, the Lumbee Indians of Robeson County.

As of early 2009 the "Cheraw Indians of the Lumber River," also known as the "Lumbee," have been given approval by the House of Representatives on a bill to grant them status as a federally recognized tribe. The Bill is now being forwarded to the Senate for a vote, if approved it most certainly will obtain the signature of the president. If the Lumbee obtain Federal recognition it will assuredly impact the social and political future of the Pee Dee of neighboring South Carolina.

The Pee Dee could use this new legal status of a tribe with such similar background to their own as a vehicle to further their own bid for Federal recognition, or more likely the Pee Dee may lose a significant number of members to the lure of federal benefits offered by membership with the Lumbee. Because a large number of the Pee Dee have a grandparent, or sibling of a grandparent, who appears on the "special Indian census" schedule claimed by the Lumbee as a base roll document, it would not be surprising if the free healthcare, employment, and housing benefits of a newly-recognized Lumbee tribe seduce away a large number of the financially stressed Pee Dee. Hopefully any change that occurs will have a positive impact on the Pee Dee, a people who have such a long and proud history in this state.

Chapter 7

The Waccamaw

Turning east from the flat farmlands of the Pee Dee, the geography slowly changes to gentle hills, dense forests, and thick swamps as one approaches the coast. Thirty miles west from the ocean on highway 501, and between the cities of Marion and Conway, the traveler will observe a brown county marker that bears "Waccamaw Tribal Grounds." This heralds the arrival at the historical homeland of the Dimery Settlement and the territory of the modern Waccamaw tribe.

Around 1810 a group of Indian families from the Marlboro-Dillon area, where they had been living less than fifteen years, migrated east to Horry County. The most prominent family among these Indians was that of John Dimery who purchased 300 acres in Horry near Dog Bluff on which would grow the seeds of the Dimery settlement. John had previously lived near Drowning Creek, present-day Robeson County, from at least 1780 to 1795 where he was taxed and appears on census schedules as a family of "Other Free Persons." John Dimery sold 350 acres of his North Carolina land sometime around 1795 and moved south where he lived for a decade among the Indians of Marlboro. John next moved east to Dog Bluff. John's brother, William Dimery, remained among the Pee Dee and was the progenitor of a host of Dimerys who appear as "Other Free

Persons," "Croatan," and "Indian" on the records of the Pee Dee.

Figure 7.1: Waccamaw Tribal Grounds Highway Sign

The 1850 census schedule reflects three Indian families living in the area of Dog Bluff: Sarah Cook, age 35, Cockren
Thompkins, age 30, his wife Elizabeth and seven children, and
John Demery, age 70, his wife Polly and nine children. John
Demery junior, who had married Elizabeth Hardwick earlier in
Marlboro, was also counted as living in the household of his
father. The birthplace and date of John Dimery senior, 1780
in North Carolina, supports his early residence in the Robeson
area.

During the Civil War hostilities the Cook, Dimery, and
Thompkins families were joined by other Indians who had
previously been living west of Horry. These included the
Ammons, Coopers, Hatchers, and Turners. The Ammons and
Turners of the Dog Bluff area descend from William Ammons
and Robert Turner, both of whom moved from Dillon to the
Dimery settlement circa 1870. An 1876 article in the Horry

News gives a "List of Colored Voters" in the November election and listed James B. Cook, George Cooper, David Dimery, J.L. Dimery, James Dimery, John Dimery, Willis Thompkins, and David Turner.

Isaac H. Hatcher, the first Hatcher to come to the Dimery settlement, had previously been living in Marlboro where David Hatcher, the founder of the Hatcher surname among the Pee Dee and Waccamaw, moved circa 1810. Earlier in history the same David Hatcher had enlisted in the North Carolina militia from the Indian settlement on Fishing Creek in Granville County. Hatcher was recorded as a "half Indian" planter on his military records. In 1905 Julius Hatcher was charged in Horry County Court with violating the law that forbade White-Black intermarriage. Hatcher was acquitted due to, as one account relates, "Absolutely no proof was made showing the presence of Negro blood in Hatcher's veins...The Hatchers are a dark-skinned people, but if there is any Negro blood in them, no one knows when or whence it got there...if anything it may be Indian or Spaniard."[1]

In 1878 the Dimery settlement formed a church on land donated by Sara Turner. Ellis Cooper, one of the Indians who helped build the church, was one of the first pastors. Originally called simply the "Dimery Church," the name was eventually changed to Bethel Missionary Baptist. Sadly the church burned to the ground in 1983, however the cemetery remains and is well kept. Another church was established in the early 1900's, which served mainly the Hatcher family. Known as the Holly Hill Free Will Baptist, this church also called many of the other Dimery families part of its congregation, and Charlie Dimery was even listed as one of the church's "head men."

The early 1900's also saw the founding of a school in the settlement. Originally called the "Dimery School," it became known in official county records as the "Pine Level School." In 1922 the families of the settlement, discovering that their school

---

[1] *Horry Herald*, Feb 16, 1905

Figure 7.2: Chief Harold "Buster" Hatcher (Waccamaw), 2009

was being funded as a Negro school, promptly refused to allow their children to attend even one more day, and sent a petition to the Horry County School Board to rectify the classification. The result was that the county agreed to fund the Pine Level School under an Indian, or "special" school classification. This seemed to pacify the Indian parents. The signers of the 1922 petition were D.W. Caines, Walter Caines, A.B. Dimery, Will Elvis, Gatlin Hatcher, Mary Hatcher, Noah Hatcher, Vander Hatcher, R.B. Nobles, and H.G. Turner. A 1949 county school survey revealed that the Pine Level School had two rooms and no running water or electricity. The school was officially closed in 1955 after enrollment declined to only nine students.

The Dimery settlement Indians, from historical times to the present, moved fluidly between Horry, Marlboro-Dillon, and

Figure 7.3: Waccamaw members celebrate purchase of tribal grounds, 2004

neighboring Robeson County. In fact, the present-day Waccamaw are no more than one or two generations removed from other Ammons, Cooper, Dimery, Hatcher and Turner families around McColl, Clio, Maxton, and Pembroke. To further illustrate this, well renowned "Lumbee Indian healer" Vernon Cooper was a nephew of Ellis Cooper, pastor of Bethel Church. Much like their neighbors the Pee Dee, the Waccamaw tribal government seems inclined to downplay any close connection to the Lumbee.[2]

Organized under the name "Waccamaw Indian People," these Indians were able to acquire twenty acres near their historic settlement, which they currently use to facilitate cultural

---

[2]Photo courtesy of Sussan Hayes Hatcher.

events and tribal gatherings. The Waccamaw were also the first tribal group to test the waters when the state approved tribal recognition criteria. In February of 2005 the Waccamaw were granted recognition as an Indian tribe by a unanimous vote of the Minority Affairs Commission. Chief Harold "Buster" Hatcher, the charismatic front man for the tribe, also serves as the Chairman of the South Carolina Indian Affairs Commission, a non-profit organization that endeavors to act as a go-between for the Governor and Carolina's Indian tribes. The Waccamaw tribal leaders have shown a desire to improve not only the social welfare of their own tribal members, but also that of all of South Carolina's Indian people, and for that they should be commended.

Chapter 8

The Catawba

In the far northeastern corner of South Carolina, a land of rich soil, thick forests, and broad rivers, lays the reservation of the Catawba Indians on the banks of the river that bears their name. The Catawba are the only tribal group that was continuously recognized as a tribal entity throughout the history of the Palmetto State, and are currently the only South Carolina tribe recognized by the United States and the Bureau of Indian Affairs. Little is known about the Catawba Tribe prior to their first encounters with Europeans.

Seventeenth Century English settlers of Savannah and Charleston were told by their Muskogean speaking Indian neighbors of a tribe of warlike Indians to the north known as the Escatawpa which meant literally "cut hair" or "scalpers" in their tongue. The "Catawba Tribe" they spoke of was actually a loose confederation of tribes who all spoke a version of the Siouan language.

Known by such general names as the Esaw, Isaw, Sara, and Saraw, this confederacy of eastern Siouan peoples included the Sugaree, Coree, Coharie, Chicoree, Congaree, Santee, Pee Dee, Wateree, Shakori, Occaneechi, Wateree, Saponi, and Tutelo among others. Encountering them in 1701, explorer John Lawson described them as "the Esaw Indians, a very large Nation, containing many thousands of people." This large Eastern Sioux confederation was soon strained by the ravages of disease and repeated raids by Iroquois who had now been provided firearms by northern white settlers. To protect themselves from enemies both human and microscopic, the mighty Esaw confederation dissolved into individual villages now separated by miles of forest and petty differences.

GROUP CATAWBA INDIANS, ROCK HILL, S. C.

Figure 8.1: Catawba Indian dance troupe, 1913 Corn Exposition, Columbia, SC

As the English settlements encroached further west into the ancestral lands of the Esaw, one small Indian band after another left their villages and joined the Catawba on their fifteen mile square reservation at the border of North and South Carolina. By 1750 the main Catawba village was bolstered by over 100 families of these refugee Indians as such tribes as the Natchez, Cusso and Yamassee moved up from the south, the Saponi and Cheraw from the north, and Waccamaw, Pee Dee, Congaree, Santee, Keyauwee, and Waterree from the eastern portions of Carolina. When James Adair traded among the Catawba villages between 1736 and 1743 he reported that he heard more than 20 different languages spoken by the Indian inhabitants.

Though surrounded by smaller remnant tribes, the Catawba reserved primary political authority and the chieftainship was retained by the purely Catawba bloodlines until the 1840's. One of this bloodline was a Catawba war Chief named New River who assumed the title 'General' as the Indians adopted a cultural practice of taking on military titles sometime between the French and Indian War and the Revolutionary War. General New River exerted supreme authority over both the Catawba and the refugee villages through all of the colonial conflicts and on into the emergence of the Nineteenth Century.

General Jacob Scott became chief of the Catawba after the death of General New River in 1801, and General Jacob Ayers succeeded him from 1821 until his own death on 14 July 1837. Ian Watson in his compilation entitled "Catawba Indian Genealogy" described the death of General Ayers in 1837 as "the end of a conservative era of Catawba tribal government.", and indeed, 3 years later the Catawba relinquished the majority of their reservation lands in South Carolina.

This shift to a more progressive thinking leadership, and the eventual self-termination of their reservation status in 1840, may have had an ethnic root instead of being the result of acculturation. Watson, Brown, and McDowell clearly identify three of the Catawba surnames as being of Cheraw origin (specifically the surnames George, Robbins, and Harris) and these families appear to have begun a push to dominate the Catawba leadership during the rule of General Ayers. The exodus of so many Catawba between 1790 and 1840 could possibly signify a reaction to the overtaking of the political structure by the mixed-blood Cheraw.

The fact that a large number of Catawba left the reservation in the fifty years between 1790 and 1840 cannot be doubted. Revolutionary enlistments and petitions of "Catawba Indians" showed the surnames Williams, Connar, Guy, Thompson, Simmons, Jones, Taylor, Cross, Cook, Bullen, Kennedy, Kelley,

Figure 8.2: Family of John Brown (Catawba) photographed by
M.R. Harrington in 1907

Young, and Dickson; surnames which do not appear after the
1820's. The Scott family, described by Brown as "a large and
prominent family" among the Catawba during their early history, supplied three men to the Revolutionary effort, Capt. Jacob
Scott, Capt. John Scott, and Billey Scott.

If these 3 males (representing at least 3 households and 12 to
25 individuals) were the only Catawba males bearing the 'Scott'
surname in 1775, then surely within sixty years the Scott family would have swollen to at least 50 individuals even by conservative estimates; yet by 1849 only two Scott individuals remained connected to the Catawba (John Scott born 1826, and
Sam Scott born 1799). By 1853, John Scott was the only individual with that surname associated with the tribe, and the
1943 Catawba Tribal roll does not bear any Catawba with the
Scott surname. Not surprisingly, this is the time period when
John and James Scott, mentioned as interpreters between the

Figure 8.3: Family of Chief David Harris (Catawba)
photographed by A.I. Robinson in 1911

Catawba Indians and the Colonial government in Charleston,
founded residences in other areas of South Carolina and their
descendants are counted among the membership of such tribes
as the Pee Dee, Santee and Sumter Cheraw.

Beginning in 1808, individual Catawba Indians began lay-
ing out plots over which they claimed personal authority, and
subsequently signed leases for these plots to white farmers. This
translated as easy money to the Catawba and the practice became so rampant that by 1840 virtually the entire reservation
was leased out and the Catawba were living in homeless squalor.
Catawba Agent J.R. Patton described them as:

> A somewhat indolent & careless people living in
> small Log Houses or cabins covered with boards
> & are not settled together in a Town or village but
> scattered over a considerable portion of the land
> they occupy they own but little furniture of any
> value a portion of them work small farms or patches
> of corn but as a general thing do not make anything
> like a support they own some Horses a few Cattle

& some Hogs. This seems to sum up the amount of what they possess.[1]

Conditions had deteriorated to the point that the vast majority of Catawba were living in North Carolina among their old enemies, the Cherokee, and other small bands were migrating to Indian Territory, the Creek Indian reservation near Atmore, Alabama, the Pamunkey reservation in Virginia, and living homeless on the fringes of white settlements in other areas of South Carolina.

By 1838 between 600 and 700 white families were holding leases and living on the Catawba reservation lands. This led to a dilemma for the South Carolina Legislature as the Catawba had difficulty collecting their rents due, the white leaseholders and their Indian landlords often disagreed as to the amount due, and even the white leaseholders argued among themselves as to boundary lines. At the inception of every disagreement all parties looked to the State government for mediation and resolution. To resolve the endless series of petitions and legal actions State representatives first toyed with the idea of changing the lease system over to a taxation process whereby taxes would be collected on the reservation leases and paid directly to the individual Indians, but finally the Legislature concluded that the easiest solution was to simply purchase the land from the Catawba.

On March 13, 1840, what few Catawba leaders that could be found, a meager five men, gathered along with state Indian commissioners at the crossroads of the Nation Ford road about a mile from the Catawba river, and signed a treaty which relinquished their title to the whole of the reservation in return for a tract of land near the Cherokee in North Carolina, $2,500 to be delivered once all of the Catawba were removed from South Carolina, and a yearly payment of $1,500 for nine more years. The state immediately was unable to abide by the conditions

---

[1]*Annual Report* of Catawba Agent J.R. Patton (1861).

of the treaty as North Carolina refused to sell any lands for the purpose of Indian relocation, and so Commissioners resorted to purchasing 630 acres in Lancaster District on the West side of the Catawba river. This purchase of land did not convince all of the Indians to return as a census taken over ten years after the Treaty of Nation Ford revealed only 54 Catawba in South Carolina and 56 still living among the Cherokee.

Figure 8.4: Family of William "Billy Bowlegs" Harris (Catawba) photographed by Speck in 1922

The Indians living on the new reservation suffered terribly as the land had been severely deforested by the previous lease-holder and their crops were repeatedly wiped out by river flood-ing. For the next 80 years Catawba leaders repetitively peti-tioned the federal government for aid to alleviate their desper-ate condition; however the United States Congress assumed the position that the Catawba were state Indians, subject to the juris-diction of South Carolina, and therefore no relationship existed between Congress and the tribe. This condition of being wards of the state existed until the 1930's when South Carolina began a campaign to transfer responsibility for the tribe over to the federal government.

In 1937, spurred by the efforts of Dr. Frank Speck, the Secretary of the Interior agreed that the federal government should re-assume responsibility for the Catawba Indians, over 3,000 more acres within their old reservation boundary were secured, and the Catawba reservation system was restored. The Indians soon learned that they had essentially traded a deaf and uncaring great white father who lived next door for an equally deaf and uncaring one who lived even farther away.

In the 1950's the United States government began a concerted effort to end the special status and ward system for Indian tribes under their jurisdiction, an era that came to be known as "Termination." Following a meeting with Congressman Robert Hemphill in 1959, the Catawba agreed to terminate their status as a federal tribe. The tribe's 3,434 acres held in trust by the Secretary of Interior were divided out among the tribal member's and, as the Catawba Termination Act stated, the Catawba became ordinary citizens of the state subject to state law and regulation "in the same manner they apply to other persons or citizens within their jurisdiction." This appeared to be the final curtain call for the Catawba; however a legal twist of fate would provide the tribe with a veritable phoenix-like revival.

In 1975 the Passamaquoddy tribe of Maine brought a lawsuit against their state arguing that the Non-Intercourse Act of 1809 made any treaty between a tribe and state government illegal unless it was approved by Congress. When the case came before the First Circuit of Appeals the Court sided with the Passamaquoddy stating in effect that not only were the treaties of Maine improper and void, but also those of many east coast states including New York, Rhode Island, Massachusetts, and South Carolina. Five years later, on October 28, 1980 the Catawba Indian Tribe of South Carolina, Inc. filed a federal class-action lawsuit for compensation of land lost due to the Treaty of Nation Ford as well as 140 years of "trespass damages." Various legal maneuverings caused the lawsuit to languish for more than a decade until the battle weary Catawba finally agreed to a settlement in 1993. Under the terms of the settlement the Catawba would have their status as a federally recognized tribe reinstated as well as receive $50 million over five years.

For the past twenty-five years the Catawba Indians have made good use of their restored federal status and settlement money. Housing grants provided shelter for elderly tribal members, a tribal governmental complex was established, and a vastly improved road system on the reservation serves almost as a symbol of better days to come. One can only hope that this new road of prosperity stretches far into the future for one of the oldest tribes in South Carolina.

Figure 8.5: Joseph Sanders (Catawba) photographed by Speck
in 1922

Index

Backintyme

30 Medford Drive
Palm Coast FL 32137-2504
860-468-9631

See our complete list of books at:
http://backintyme.com/publishing.php

Order extra copies of this book at:
http://backintyme.com/ad405.php

Made in the USA
Columbia, SC
16 June 2020

11158210R00057